CONTENTS

The covers and inside front and back pages show the author and her model, an immature jenday conure. The title page shows the author teaching the conure to climb from finger to finger.

Distributed in the UNITED STATES by T.F.H. Publications, Inc., 211 West Sylvania Avenue, Neptune City, NJ 07753; in CANADA by H & L Pet Supplies Inc., 27 Kingston Crescent, Kitchener, Ontario N2B 2T6; Rolf C. Hagen Ltd., 3225 Sartelon Street, Montreal 382 Quebec; in ENGLAND by T.F.H. (Great Britain) Ltd., 11 Ormside Way, Holmethorpe Industrial Estate, Redhill, Surrey RH1 2PX; in AUSTRALIA AND THE SOUTH PACIFIC by T.F.H. (Australia) Pty. Ltd., Box 149, Brookvale 2100 N.S.W., Australia; in NEW ZEALAND by Ross Haines & Son, Ltd., 18 Monmouth Street, Grey Lynn, Auckland 2 New Zealand; in SINGAPORE AND MALAYSIA by MPH Distributors Pte., 71-77 Stamford Road, Singapore 0617; in the PHILIPPINES by Bio-Research, 5 Lippay Street, San Lorenzo Village, Makati, Rizal; in SOUTH AFRICA by Multipet Pty. Ltd., 30 Turners Avenue, Durban 4001. Published by T.F.H. Publications Inc., Ltd., the British Crown Colony of Hong Kong. THIS IS THE 1983 EDITION.

TAMING AND TRAINING
CONURES

by RISA TEITLER
Professional Trainer

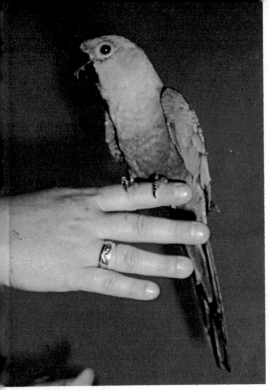

Consult your local pet shop and try to buy a young conure (left) which is already tame. If you have other pets in your home, like a cat (below), be sure of the safety of the conure against a "sneak attack."

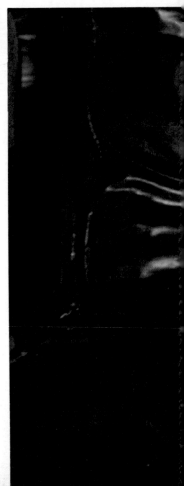

Introduction

This book is intended for people who are shopping for their first pet conure and do not have a clear idea of how to attempt the taming, socialization and care of their new bird. Most, by far, pet conures are bought from retail shops, and that is the best place to begin looking for your pet conure. Breeders of conures are not easily found.

The size of these birds and their attractive coloration make them a desirable choice for many prospective buyers. They are adaptable and hardy and in many respects behave like their larger cousins, the macaws.

All conures have the potential to mimic speech, and some make excellent talkers. Most have an inexhaustible ability

to entertain with natural antics or learned behaviors. Most species are inexpensive, and there usually is a large selection of species readily available.

The chapters entitled "Choosing a Healthy, Trainable Bird " and "Taming a Wild Conure" were written for motivated bird owners. A great deal can be accomplished with a logical training regime.

ABOUT THE MODEL

The model used for most of the pictures in this book is an immature jenday conure. This bird was bought from an importer when it was approximately three months old. I discovered that it required supplemental feeding with softfood because it did not crack seed efficiently and began to lose weight quickly.

I fed the bird by hand three times daily. During the feedings I talked to the bird and, to my surprise, within two weeks the conure was beginning to speak! In one month the bird not only said the word hello clearly, but he also said it on command!

In another two weeks new words were being practiced. He seemed to mimic everything he heard from the other birds in my house. It became necessary to give speech lessons that concentrated on one word or phrase at a time to keep the conure from becoming confused.

I do not think that this bird is exceptional among conures, but compared to the other conures I have handled, it is certainly a fast learner.

At the same time that this bird began talking, it began to exhibit many behaviors that could be modified into simple tricks. By grabbing my fingers with one foot, for instance, it would try to roll over backwards. Very soon I began teaching this bird to do a headstand before each feeding.

It should be mentioned that this conure was a fairly wild bird when first acquired. Although he was very young, he bit every time he was approached. The biting behavior

8

The model used for most of the photographs in this book is an immature jenday conure shown to the left. The author, below, taught this bird to speak within two weeks!

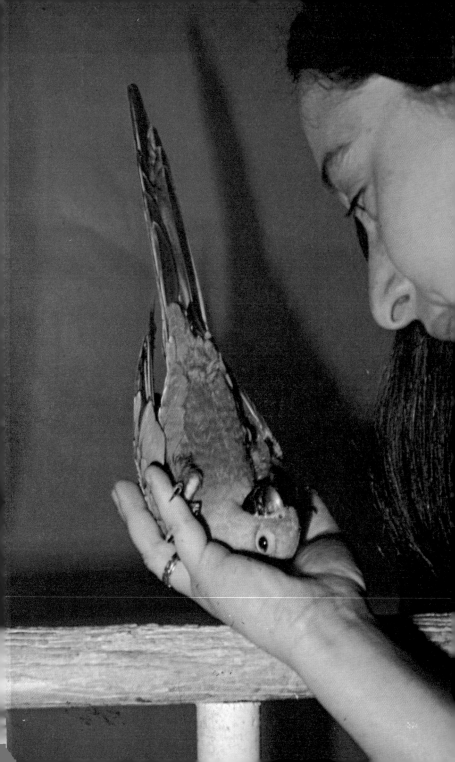

The conure shown above bit the author every time she handled it, but it soon loved her so much it developed an inexhaustible craving for her attention.

Anyone who spends enough time with a conure can expect good progress in taming, speech acquisition and simple trick training, as shown by the author and her model (left).

Offer the conure food rewards while conducting the lessons, but don't expect it to continue training while it is feeding on the reward. You can, of course, pet it and talk to it while it feeds (see photos below).

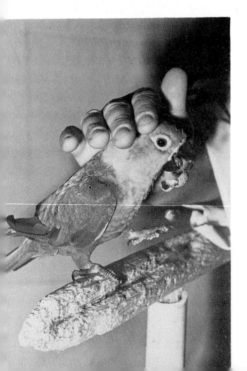

soon ended and was replaced by an inexhaustible craving for attention—attention not only from me but also from my husband, my friends and my neighbors.

I would like to emphasize that this is not an exceptional conure. It did require more attention than most new birds because it lacked ability to crack enough seeds to keep up its weight. But anyone who spends enough time with their new conure can expect similar progress in taming, speech acquisition and simple trick training.

Good luck with your new conure. Be patient and consistent, and you will very likely be as surprised and delighted with your new pet conure as I was with mine.

CONURES IN GENERAL

Conures are, first of all, members of the large order of birds commonly known as parrots. There are several genera and many different species of conures. The whole South American continent is inhabited by conures, and they also are found in Mexico, Central America and the islands of the Caribbean. Some have been well known as caged pets for years, while others are just beginning to find their way to the pet trade of the United States. The increasing interest in conures as pet birds is due to their diversity in size, lively personalities, availability and reasonable cost.

Conures are classified into seven genera: *Aratinga, Nandayus, Leptosittacea, Ognorhynchus, Cyanoliseus, Pyrrhura* and *Enicognathus*. They range in size from approximately seven inches to twenty inches in total length. Their tails are tapered, but the length of the tail differs according to species. All have fairly large heads with noticeable periophthalmic rings. The eye ring may be white, yellow, beige or black, while the iris of the eye may be a brilliant gold, yellow or black. Often the contrast between the color of the eye ring and the iris gives a conure a dramatic, striking appearance.

You should train your conure to perch on a training stick as early as possible. Should he fly onto a high perch on top of your windows or doors, or should it fly into a tree, the ease with which you can retrieve him with a stick makes such training mandatory.

Training the conure to perch on a stick begins with gently shoving the stick against its breast (see facing page) in such a manner that unless it grabs the stick it will be pushed off the perch. Once it grabs the perch with one foot, the other will soon follow with just a bit more pressure.

15

Some conures (the golden conure, *Aratinga guarouba*, for example) have a massive beak in a proportionately small face; others (like the Patagonian conure, *Cyanoliseus patagonus*) have a small beak in a large face. Beak color also differs with the species and can be black, yellow or beige.

The wings are broad and enable the conures to be very strong, swift flyers. General plumage varies from predominantly green to bright yellow-gold; many species also display shades of red, orange, brown, blue, lavender and maroon. Some do, indeed, look as though they were inspired by a creative artist.

The species of conures most common in captivity include the small orange-fronted (Petz's) conure, *Aratinga canicularis*, from Central America and Mexico, the large Patagonian conure from South America and the medium-sized nanday conure, *Nandayus nenday*, also from South America. These species are different in size and coloration, yet all can be found at a reasonable cost at local pet shops. Other conures that are gaining popularity as caged pets are the beautifully colored sun and jenday conures, *Aratinga solstitialis* and *A. jandaya*. There are many more conure species that make fine pets or aviary subjects, and they will undoubtedly find their way to the retail market in coming years.

There is no sexual dimorphism in any of the conure species; in other words, both males and females attain identical plumage. Immature birds resemble the adults and therefore are difficult to differentiate from them. The nesting behavior of certain conures is very interesting. The Patagonian, for example, builds or, more accurately, digs its nest into the side of a cliff. There it makes a burrow with a small chamber at the end of a tunnel (more like a den than a nest).

Worth mentioning here is the only parrot native to the mainland of the United States, now extinct. This bird, the Carolina parakeet, was a close relative of members of the

A couple of Finsch's conures, Aratinga finschi. *Photo by Louise Van der Meid from* Parrots and Related Birds, *a large encyclopedic work published by T.F.H. Publications.*

After teaching the conure to get onto the training stick, you must train him to get off it and onto the perch. Start by holding the stick and perch on the same level and then push the conure gently with your hand until it leaves the stick.

The conure to the left is a maroon-bellied, while the birds shown below are a couple of scarlet-fronted conures, Aratinga wagleri. *Photos by Louise Van der Meid.*

genus *Aratinga*. Once widely distributed from New York to Southern Florida, west to Colorado and the Dakotas, the Carolina parakeet was last officially reported in a sighting in the marshlands of Florida.

The decline of the Carolina parakeet correlates with the continuing development of land for commercial or residential use. These birds traveled in flocks of two to three hundred and showed no fear of man. They were easy to shoot while alighting in fruit trees to eat. Although many were shot by irate farmers, the evidence indicates that the flocks were destroyed not by predation but by destruction of the natural habitat of the birds.

At present, this same pattern of destruction of habitat and decline of parrot species is being repeated in South America. It is not likely that this land development will diminish. As the many species of parrots (including conures) which are desirable for pets are considered to be valuable natural resources by the countries involved, they will probably be captured and sold to the pet trade. It is hoped that at least some of these birds will be placed into controlled breeding situations to ensure their continued survival.

It should be pointed out that not all of the parrots in South America have declined in populated areas. The spunky nanday conure, which inhabits a large area including parts of Argentina, Bolivia, Brazil and Paraguay, has actually increased in numbers in populated areas. Nandays have been observed nesting and successfully rearing young in hollow fence posts of farms and small communities.

Conures, like other members of the parrot family, have a fairly long life expectancy. Longevity is influenced by diet and environment, but generally speaking, a lifespan of twenty to thirty-five years is not unrealistic.

The voice quality of many conures is loud and raucous. They have the capacity for imitating speech, and some are

Conures are American parrots (from South and Central America). They have tapered tails (see the conure above) and rings around their eyes (see facing page.)

excellent mimics. Keep in mind that teaching a conure to speak is not a simple task. It requires patience and organization on the trainer's part. The potential for speech also varies with each species.

The great majority of conures are tamable and trainable. I consider taming in a different light from training. Taming involves the most basic lessons that your conure must learn: eating from your hand, sitting on a stand and hand training. The training of a conure cannot begin until the preliminaries of taming are accomplished.

The two sources from which to obtain a conure are either a reliable retail pet shop or a private breeder. A pet shop is really the best source because the experienced personnel are always available for help and there is a wide selection of birds and supplies. The private breeder is often difficult to locate and usually does not sell the food and accessories that you will require for your new pet. Large department stores often sell pet birds, but such establishments offer little selection and cannot give you any experienced advice.

The reputable retail shop is also your best source for an adequate cage and stand for your conure. The single pet can be comfortable in a standard parrot cage, approximately twenty-four inches square and thirty inches high. Pairs of birds or small community groups must be housed in larger cages with room enough for free flight, if breeding is considered.

Most conures are very hardy, healthy birds. Rarely should you encounter serious health problems if you follow the procedures in this book for feeding and care. There are no required immunizations for parrots, but it is advisable to locate an experienced avian vet before the need arises. Write the vet's telephone number and address in your family phone directory. Also locate an alternate vet to call if you cannot contact your first choice.

The personality of your new pet conure can be described as a cross between a macaw and a lovebird. In many ways conures are like tiny macaws! They are noisy, curious and playful. Their cage and stand often double as gymnasiums as with very little prompting they perform their acrobatic routines.

Conures are clever birds and quickly master most of the tasks that a trainer attempts to teach. They are sociable birds with a strong pecking order. In other words, do not place a new bird in the same cage or aviary with birds that are established residents. The new bird will be subjected to pecking by the other birds, no matter what its age or sex. In some cases a new bird may be pecked to death. It is possible to integrate new birds into established settings, but this should be done carefully, keeping a close watch on the birds.

Conures form possessive attitudes toward both objects and people. Family pets can become favorite friends of your conure, but interaction should always be supervised. Your dog or cat may not understand the affectionate nip of your conure until they have been together for some time.

Conures are clever birds and quickly learn most tricks that their master attempts to teach them. This one is playing dead.

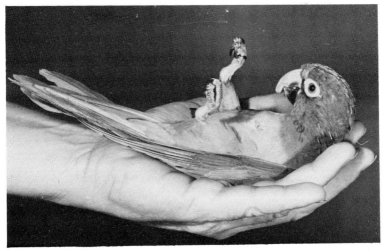

The author spreads the wings on her model. These wings have had many feathers clipped to prevent the bird from flying.

On the facing page, the author demonstrates how long the feathers would have been were they not clipped. Clipping the bird's flight feathers is neither painful nor dangerous if done correctly.

When buying a bird from a pet shop or anywhere else, be sure the bird looks healthy and has all its feathers (see the photo below). If possible, get one (left) which allows you to touch it without biting you.

Choosing a Healthy, Trainable Bird

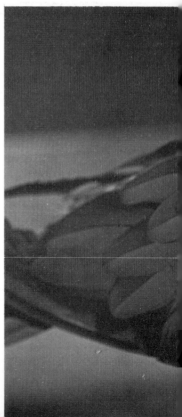

You should examine any bird before you purchase it. This examination will help to determine if the conure is healthy. It is always easier to care for a healthy bird than it is to nurse a sick one back to good health. A healthy conure is active. It moves about the cage with ease, using both feet to grip the wire as it climbs. Have a pet shop employee remove the bird from the cage so you can look at it more closely.

The plumage should be smooth and even. No bare skin should be visible anywhere on the bird. Some feathers of the wing and tail may be bent or broken. This should be of little concern unless the whole tail and most of the feathers of a wing are missing or broken. By all means, look for a bird with better plumage. Also, any conure that sits with its feathers fluffed should not be purchased.

The eyes and eye rings should be examined closely.

The author introduces her jenday conure to her pet Amazon parrot. She must always be careful not to allow birds the chance to attack each other.

On the facing page is a conure which has been properly clipped. Most of its flight feathers have been cut, preventing the conure from flying away from training.

When selecting your bird, examine it carefully. It should never show any bald spots or naked spots where the skin shows through. Examine the feet. Each foot should have four toes, two extending forward and two backward.

Healthy eyes are bright and alert. Dull, watery eyes may be symptomatic of illness. Eye rings should have no scabs, sores or irritations of any type. No matter how minor a scratch on the eye ring may appear to you in the excitement of obtaining a new pet, you should reject any bird with eye problems.

The nasal openings of a healthy bird are clean and free of debris. Discharge from the nose is not acceptable in a new pet.

Examine the feet. There should be four toes on each foot. Two toes normally extend forward and two backward when gripping the perch. Take the time to observe the bird's grip on a perch. Birds with broken or missing toes are usually more difficult to hand train. There should be one claw at the end of each toe. One absent claw is no serious disability, but many missing claws may be.

The skin of the legs should not be lumpy or have overgrown scales. Both feet and legs should feel equally warm to your touch. If one foot is very hot or very cold, the bird may have a medical problem.

The vent should be clean and pink in color. There should be no soiling on the feathers surrounding the vent.

Observe the bird's respiration. Healthy birds have slow, even respiration. Rapid or irregular breathing should alert you to possible illness.

Also look carefully at the feces on the cage bottom. Normal fecal matter has solid form and is dark green and white when dry. A watery or off-color stool disqualifies any conure, no matter how healthy it appears in other ways. Off-color stools are brown, yellowish or slightly orange. Black, tarry feces are also abnormal.

When a bird seems to pass all of these tests for health, feel the breast. It is imperative that your choice have "good weight." This means that the breastbone has ample flesh on either side and does not protrude. Thin birds are certain to have medical problems. Do not purchase any thin bird.

Even though you buy a tame conure, it must have a cage. It can't stay perched on your hand (left) all the time, but must have a perch of its own (below).

Housing and Feeding

You must have an adequate cage for the conure before bringing it home. The best cage for a single pet is one made of metal. The smallest acceptable dimensions are twenty inches square and twenty-six to thirty inches high. Anything smaller will cramp a conure. Keep in mind that they are very active birds, with a propensity for chewing. Cages constructed of wood or bamboo, no matter how beautiful, will not hold the bird for long.

Plastic cage-tops are not recommended because most conures enjoy hanging from the top of their cage while playing. Plastic bottom trays are less desirable than metal. Painted metal will chip before long and lose its nice appearance.

The best cages are nickel-plated and have a silvery finish. You may prefer the same cage with a gold finish. Both are usually available at well-stocked retail stores.

Bottom grills are useful for keeping the conure out of its own debris. These grills should be removable for easy cleaning. Other accessories include food and water dishes, perches, swings and toys. Most cages come equipped with food cups, perches and swing. Good materials for the food dishes are hard plastic, plexiglass and ceramic-surfaced clay. Plain clay is not recommended. Metal dishes are fine for food but less desirable for water. Glass is very clean, but it does break.

The best perches are made of natural wood branches. Dowels are fine, but they do not offer the advantage of varying gripping surfaces. You may decide to replace the dowel perch with a branch. Be sure that you use only untreated wood from living trees. You can use citrus wood, oak, ficus, pine, olive or mango. Do not use wood from trees that have thick sap, and do not use any wood that you are uncertain about.

At this point it is appropriate to caution against allowing the conure to chew the leaves of houseplants. Not all varieties of houseplants are harmful to birds, but many are.

TOYS

When choosing toys for your conure there are a few basic guidelines which you should follow. Never give bells with flimsy clappers, or any other toy with poorly attached parts. Wood, metal and hard plastic are fine materials for toys. Avoid giving mirrors or other toys with reflective surfaces, especially if you plan to attempt speech training. Your bird may become more interested in its own reflected image than in what you are attempting to teach it. Do not crowd the cage with toys. Playgrounds have become increasingly popular and are available at many retail pet shops. Do not allow the conure unlimited freedom in a

Cages for all parrots should be made of strong metal with heavy wire so the bird can't bite through it.

If you can't afford a large cage for your birds, you can make one of heavy wire mesh, like the one shown above. On the facing page, the top picture shows an excellent parrot cage. Pet birds (facing page, lower photo) must never be allowed to eat houseplants, as many are poisonous or have been sprayed with poison.

Conures must have room and should not be cramped or they will fight. One conure to a cage this large is enough.

playground, or you will have a more difficult time taming and training it. Sturdy chains and certain dog bones are fine chew toys. Whatever toy you decide to provide, teach the conure to play with you before its toys.

Never suspend any toy from a string in the center of the bird cage. Birds have a way of tangling themselves in dangling string. (By the same token, be sure that there are no stray threads hanging from the cage cover, if you use one.)

One of the best toys that I have ever found is a small piece of soft wood with a hole drilled in it and attached to the side of the cage. You can make these yourself from untreated lumber, replacing them as necessary.

You may find that your bird will enjoy a game of tug with a short piece of light chain and with you as the opponent.

Try to select toys that can be used in trick training, if that is your goal.

CAGE PLACEMENT

The placement of your bird's cage in the house is important. Family pets are happiest when close to the mainstream of family activity. The kitchen is a poor choice, for temperatures may fluctuate greatly. The dining or family rooms are excellent spots for the cage.

For those people who live in warm climates, the cage may be placed outdoors, shielded from direct sun, while the family is recreating on the porch. Be certain not to leave the conure outdoors unattended, unless there is adequate security from neighborhood pets. Never leave your bird outdoors alone on a bird stand.

Keep the cage away from air conditioning, fans, radiators and heating outlets. Placement near the front or back door is not recommended. You may find that the cage must be moved in winter in order to keep the conure out of drafts.

Remember that permanent cage placement comes after basic taming is accomplished. Before that, you may find it necessary to move the cage into a prepared taming area or

Conures need
mineral supplements
which they can get
either from cut-
tlebone (shown to
the left) or from
mineral blocks
(below).

If your conure enjoys raw fruit, he can be rewarded with a piece of fresh apple with the skin removed. Your pet shop will have many vitamin, mineral and oil supplements available for your pet conure (see below).

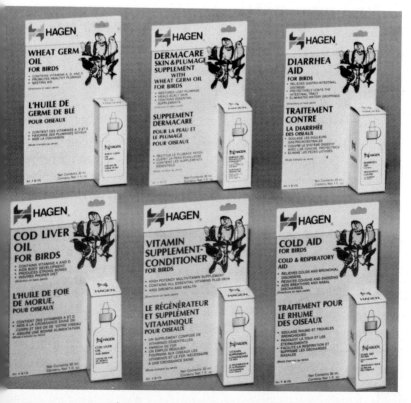

to keep it in a quiet room until the bird has mastered the basics. If you are an infrequent teacher, however, do not deprive your conure of company by keeping it isolated in a side room.

FEEDING

Feeding the conure can be fairly simple or very complex, depending upon you. The best diet is one that is well balanced and simple to provide. The following diet can be administered to a single pet or to an aviary full of conures; it is a maintenance diet only.

Sunflower seed, with parakeet mix and oats added
Raw peanuts
Raw fruit
Raw vegetables
Green leafy vegetables
Mineral block or cuttlebone, placed in the cage and
   replaced periodically
Vitamin, mineral and oil supplements
Gravel (optional)

Buy your sunflower seed, parakeet mix and all other supplies from a feed store or your bird shop. The quality of seed is important in maintaining the bird's good health. You may try other small seeds including safflower, hemp and niger, but these are not imperative in a maintenance diet.

Give a measured amount of seed each day to keep track of the conure's normal daily intake. When you notice that the bird's intake changes suddenly, either a marked increase in food consumption or a definite decrease, you should begin observing other facets of the bird's behavior. Changes in food intake are often symptomatic of illness. One day of change is not alarming, but two or three days should clue you to suspect something out of the ordinary. A change in appetite means that the bird's nutritional requirements are different from before. You may find that your conure is ready to lay eggs, or it may be molting. Remember that normal molting occurs in late summer and in spring. Feather loss at other times of the year should be watched carefully.

Raw peanuts can be given in the food dish or held back and used for taming and training. Dry-roasted, salted peanuts are not recommended as bird food. Limit the number of peanuts given each day. Two to four are fine, but ten are too many.

Fruit sprinkled with vitamin and mineral supplements should be provided daily. Suggested fruits include apples, oranges (feed citrus sparingly), bananas, berries, grapes, melons and other fruits in season.

Vegetables that can be fed each day include raw corn, peas, green beans, squash, cucumber and carrots among others.

Do not overfeed fruits and vegetables. A good formula is one green and one yellow vegetable, two fruits and one small slice of citrus (the citrus is optional). The conure may not accept these foods at first, but usually the fruit and vegetable portions will shortly be relished.

A green leafy vegetable should be given daily. Use escarole, chicory, romaine, turnip tops or carrot tops. As with all fruits and vegetables, raw is best. Raw fruits and vegetables provide the most nutrients.

Vitamin, mineral and oil supplements should also be provided for your conure. There are many products on the market and available at your local pet shop. For proper use, follow the directions on the product package.

Gravel has always been provided to my birds in a separate dish. The hens seem to eat a great deal of gravel prior to laying. There is controversy among bird keepers concerning the wisdom of providing gravel; some feel that it can be the cause of impacted gizzard. Although this has not been my experience, readers may choose to provide

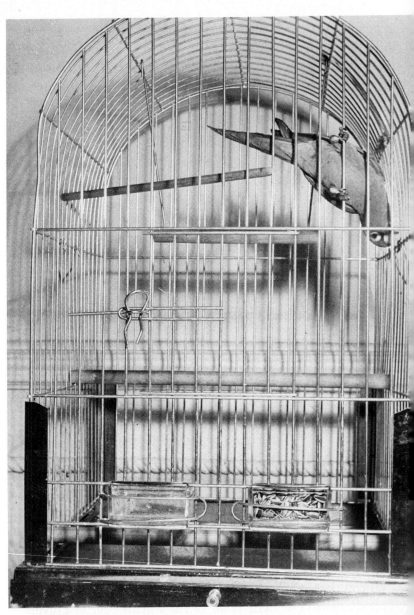

This parrot cage has water and seed dishes that are removable without allowing the parrot a chance for escape. This is especially necessary when you ask a neighbor to feed your birds while you are on vacation.

The author raises many conures. Like these plum-headed parakeets, she hand-feeds them, as this is the best way to ensure that the birds will be perfectly tame and easily trained by the novice bird owner. There is no substitution for hand-feeding if you want a great pet conure.

gravel just one week out of the month or even less often if preferred. However, a mineral supplement should be given daily to take the place of the lost source of minerals.

Sick, convalescing, very young or very old birds must be fed foods which will provide more calories in a form easily absorbed. Also, birds that are expected to reproduce should have a particularly nutritious diet high in calories. Additional softfoods and the use of all suggested supplements are recommended.

The success you can expect in taming and training your conure lies more in your ability than in the bird's ability. You must be self-confident and have lots of time. The author, shown below, spends every day, hours at a time, with a single bird.

Taming a Wild Conure

Only one person should teach the conure the basics of tame behavior; more than one person will confuse the new bird. Only when a bird has learned to eat seed from the hand of one person and perch on his or her hand without biting can a second person begin working with the bird.

The best candidate for doing the initial work with a new conure is a person with self-confidence, personal organization and dedication to the task. The initial taming may take a short time or a very long time, so it is imperative that the trainer have ample time to devote on a daily basis.

When your conure doesn't resent a little help getting from perch to stick, you'll soon be able to move on to handling.

Conures don't enjoy being nudged from the rear, but they can become accustomed to it, especially if you use it for short moves from perch to stick.

After the conure has been trained to perch on a stick and then leave the stick, you can begin to handle it.

Mature children can accomplish taming with the smaller conures, but it is not wise to leave the task to a child under twelve years of age. If the conure is a very wild individual, think twice before expecting a twelve-year-old to tame it.

The sex of the trainer is not important in the beginning lessons, but if, say, a woman handles the conure to the exclusion of all others, it is possible that the bird will have a bias toward women.

A taming area should be set aside in a quiet part of your home. A small room with few articles of furniture is your best bet. The taming area should be equipped with a low bird stand, a carpeted or padded floor and one long and two short training sticks.

You may have purchased a bird net from your pet shop. It is useful in an emergency, but a net is not a tool to use in taming a wild bird. In a pinch, a large towel can be used as effectively as a net to capture and restrain a bird, but do not use a towel as a method of taming.

Gloves are thought by many to be a necessary piece of equipment for taming. I disagree. People that work carefully and slowly do not get bitten very often. Gloves do little to protect you from the bite of a terrified conure, but if you must have them, buy tight-fitting golf gloves in a flesh tone. Red or pink gloves will alarm a wild bird.

A four-foot-high bird stand is fine for both taming and free time outside the cage once the conure is tame. A natural wood crossbar is best, but a dowel one inch to one-and-a-half inches in diameter will do. Your training sticks should be of the same diameter, one inch to one-and-a-half inches. The long stick is good for retrieving the conure from high places and should be two-and-a-half to three feet long. The shorter sticks should be between one and one-and-one-half feet long. I suggest having two, even though only one is used at a time. When you're working with your conure, you may put one stick down somewhere and then not be able to find it. It's nice to have a second handy.

CLIPPING WINGS

Clipping one wing can help expedite the taming process. Many people feel that wing clipping is inhumane; I assure you, it is not. Consider the possibility that a flighted bird may be so difficult to tame that you give up trying and confine it to a cage. A wing-clipped bird tames down fairly quickly and can enjoy the freedom of a bird stand outside of the cage. Wing clipping is far more humane than chaining the leg of your conure to a stand. Leg chains should *never* be used if you plan to follow the methods suggested in this book.

Clip only one wing. This will discourage the bird from flying because no matter in what direction it aims when taking off, it does not land facing that direction. With both wings clipped it is more likely that the conure will be able to travel in a chosen direction.

It is best to have all of your equipment assembled before capturing the bird. This will minimize the length of time you have to restrain the bird. The necessary equipment for wing clipping includes a pair of small wire cutters, a good pair of scissors, good light, styptic powder and a steady person to assist you. Never attempt to clip a bird if you have not observed an experienced person performing the procedure.

To capture the conure either place a towel over the bird or use a net designed for bird catching. With the net or towel over the bird's head, grasp it firmly but carefully behind the head and around the neck. Have your assistant remove the feet from the material by freeing the claws and holding both feet with one or two fingers between the legs. Use your other hand to keep the wings from flapping dangerously against any hard surface.

With the feet under control, slip a hand around the bird's head and remove it from the net. Keep your thumb under the lower mandible to prevent the bird from biting. If using a capture towel, you may find it advantageous to keep the bird's head wrapped in the towel. Be careful not to smother the bird.

With the bird under control, the holder should restrain it against a prepared (padded) counter or his towel-covered lap.

Under good light, the person who is doing the clipping should examine each wing. Holding the wing at the bend to prevent injury, look at the feathers. If one wing is fully feathered and one shows some breakage, clip the one with broken feathers. Leave the better feathered wing alone.

Learn to identify blood feathers (new feathers) before you begin to clip. Blood feathers are feathers that have not finished growing. They are fed by a blood supply through the quill that couples within the follicle to the internal vascular system. If a blood feather is cut, broken or cracked, it will bleed until the blood clots or the feather is removed. Have someone show you the difference between blood feathers and fully grown feathers.

If you have any doubts about identifying blood feathers, *do not clip the wing.*

With the under wing-coverts pushed back to expose feather quills, you should be able to clearly see if any blood feathers are present. Conures are strong flyers, so a fairly heavy clip is recommended. Leave the first two feathers on the end of the wing alone. With scissors, cut the third feather straight across the quill, leaving about one-third of the feather emerging from the wing.

Use the wire cutters to clip the next ten feathers. Be certain to leave at least one-and-a-half to two inches of quill to prevent any injury to the wing. With one wing clipped, a wild bird will probably take a couple of falls during the first few lessons, but it will soon settle down.

Sometimes it becomes necessary to clip a few feathers from the second wing if the conure continues to fly even though one wing is clipped. It is not recommended that you clip both wings to begin with, but if you find that the bird

Clipping a bird's wing is better than chaining its foot. Clip about eleven feathers on one wing as described in the text.

The photo above shows approximately how much to cut, while the photo at the left shows the conure after its wing feathers have been cut.

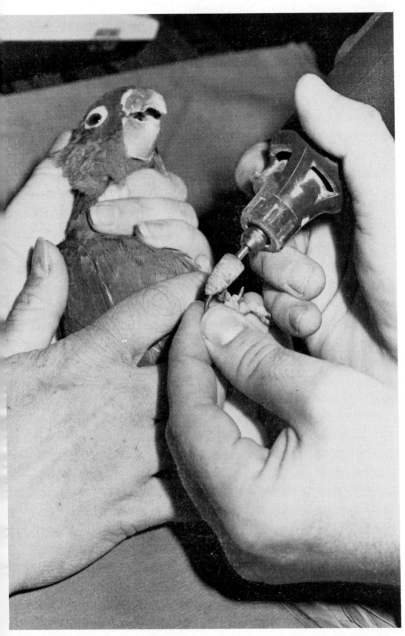

To file the claws, you should have someone hold the bird while you carefully follow the instructions in the text.

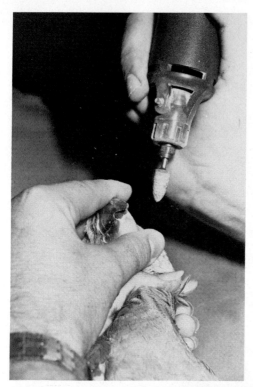

It is rare that you have to grind down the beak of a conure since they use the beak for climbing. But should your conure split its beak, causing it to grow abnormally, then a veterinarian with experience in treating birds should grind it smooth.

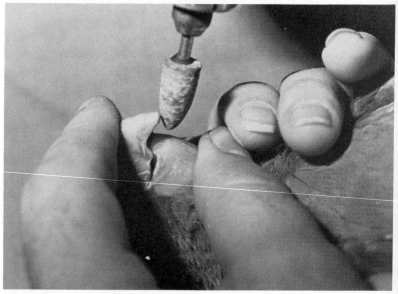

refuses to settle down, you should trim a bit of the second wing. Extend the unclipped wing. Leave the first three feathers as they are. Using your small wire cutters, clip four or five feathers, leaving at least two inches of quill protruding from the edge of the wing to protect it. *Do not clip more than five feathers* on the second wing.

When you release the bird, place it feet down on the floor or inside a cage. Release the feet first and then the head. Never drop a wild newly clipped conure. Do not place it on a counter or table top either. When you release the bird on the floor, be ready to begin stick training it.

CLIPPING CLAWS

When you are finished clipping the wing, you may want to clip the claws. But if the wild conure begins to show a great deal of distress from being restrained, you may have to skip nail clipping until another time. The signs of distress that you should look out for are choking, extremely rapid breathing and pupils that fail to respond to light.

As with wing clipping, have an experienced person show you the procedure. Also, have all your equipment assembled before you begin. To perform a pedicure on the claws you will need wire cutters or dog nail trimmers (I don't like the way scissors cut claws). An emery board or metal nail file is good for filing the claws smooth. Have styptic powder on hand in case you cut into the vein. Work in good light.

Capture and hold the conure in the same manner as for wing clipping. You may find it helpful to use a towel to wrap the wings. This will keep them from flapping. The holder should hold both legs in one hand with two fingers between the legs. The person doing the clipping then isolates each toe and carefully clips the tip of the claw. Be very careful that you don't clip too much off. You can cut more if you take too little, but you can't replace anything once it's cut. Clip all four toenails on one foot before going on to the other foot. After clipping all eight claws, file each one.

If at any time you hit blood, stop clipping and apply styptic powder. Press a small amount of the powder into the bleeding spot. When bleeding is very heavy, use cotton to press the powder into the claw. Keep pressure on the wound for three minutes. As soon as possible place the bird back into its cage. Wait two days before finishing the pedicure, and make sure the wound is healed before you attempt to tame the bird. People that work carefully rarely clip the nails to the point of bleeding. Do not panic if you hit blood. Just use the styptic powder and then leave the bird alone. The blood of most birds clots well in a short time.

With the clipping complete, release the conure into your prepared taming area. Have your training sticks and the bird stand ready. Try to let the bird become accustomed to its lack of flight for a few minutes. This is best accomplished with the bird on the floor.

THE FIRST LESSON

The first lesson should concentrate on teaching the bird to perch on a stick. Some birds are very quick and learn to perch on a stick in the first lesson. Others take longer. Some avoid the stick and flap away at your approach.

Move slowly toward the bird and present the stick as you kneel down on the floor. Stay low to the floor as you coax the bird to step onto the stick. If it puts one foot on the stick and leaves one on the floor, that's fine for starters. Your ultimate goal is to teach the bird to step up on the stick, remain there and step off when you lower the stick.

Once your conure willingly steps onto the stick, rise slowly until you are standing with the bird. At first don't move. Let the bird feel secure before you begin moving around the room. At this point you can place the bird on its stand. Take a five-minute break.

Now work on having the conure step from the stand to the stick. Let it sit on the stick for a minute and then place it back on the stand.

If the bird jumps away from the stick or stand, slowly move toward the bird and retrieve it with a stick. Begin your drill again.

When your conure is resting on its stand, offer bits of food from your hand. Try peanuts, sunflower seeds, apple, banana or any other item from the bird's normal diet. Many birds at first throw away these food rewards, but most learn to appreciate the treat.

HAND TRAINING

With some conures, you may feel ready in a very short time to start hand training. Be a good observer and decide when to begin substituting your hand for the training stick. If you have a very nervous conure, put plenty of time into the stick-and-stand drills before offering your hand.

I do not believe that you must let a bird bite you to show it that it can't hurt you. Of course it hurts! Most birds do not bite you aggressively anyway, so to "show no fear" has no value. It is far better to work slowly and never get bitten than to wear gloves, rush the bird and receive a few good bites.

Try not to overreact if you get bitten. Use your free hand to distract the bird's attention whenever you offer your hand. (It is good to begin using your free hand during stick training.) Use your voice to startle the bird if it gets a good hold on you. A loud NO should startle the bird into letting go. A distracting movement by your free hand should also divert its attention and make it release its hold.

Do not strike the bird or grab it to pull its beak off your hand. As soon as the bird feels your free hand on or around its wings, it will bite you for all it's worth. Remember, most birds bite from fear. Grabbing will surely frighten the tiny creature.

*Wild conures must trust
their handlers before they
stop being aggressive. This
takes time, just as do
human friendships and
relationships.*

*After training your conure
to step from your hand to
its stand and back, you can
train it to step from hand
to hand.*

*You should spend time
walking around with your
conure on your hand, but
restrict this walk to the
training area until the
relationship between you
and your bird is secure.*

62

Let the bird settle down a minute if it bites you. Do not end a lesson when you have been bitten. If necessary go back to stick work to end the lesson on a high note. Some birds will nip you as you hand them bits of food. If this is the case, use larger pieces of food; for example, whole peanuts in the shell or a large slice of apple. Eventually the bird will see that the food is a treat and will stop nipping you.

Wild birds must begin to trust their human handlers before they can drop their aggressive "fronts." You cannot rush a bird into trusting you, but you can speed up the process by giving your taming lessons every day, always presenting the material in the same manner. Slow movements and soft speech help the process.

When hand training the bird, the first drill should be in stepping onto the stand from your hand and then back to your hand. Before you take it from the taming area, make sure that the bird will step onto your hand. You should also spend time walking in the taming area with the conure on your hand. When you do feel ready, walk slowly to an adjoining room. Do not venture far at first. Talk to the bird and try to keep it facing you. This will discourage it from jumping.

These are the basics of tame behavior. A motivated trainer can usually accomplish this taming in less than two weeks. Always remember that some birds can take much longer. If you are a diligent trainer, you will soon see progress.

It is recommended that you teach the conure to sit on your hand and remain there before allowing it to climb up to your shoulder. Birds usually seek the highest available perch for security. To keep the bird from climbing up your arm, use your free hand to block it. Place your hand in front of the bird, the palm perpendicular to your arm. This usually works well. If the bird gets to your shoulder, use a stick to get it down, until it is willing to step right onto your hand. Some birds can be very possessive of a shoulder perch and will bite when you try to take them down.

Once your conure is hand trained, you may wish to pet the bird. Most conures will gradually learn to accept and enjoy being petted, but petting should not be forced on them.

HELPFUL HINTS

When you are just beginning the taming of a wild conure, it is advisable to remove any necklaces, earrings or other jewelry. Wear clothing that will not snag the bird's claws.

The length and frequency of your lessons will depend upon your normal daily schedule. Try to give the bird *at least* two hours of your attention each day. Use the time to actually work with the bird. Free time out of the cage does not count as work time.

This does not mean that you spend two straight hours taming or training a wild conure. Break up the time into fifteen minute sessions. Work for fifteen minutes on the appropriate drill. Then let the bird relax on its stand. Go back and repeat the lesson for fifteen minutes each time you can during the day or evening.

People who are home all day should spend as much time as possible working with the bird. Do not restrict yourself to two hours of work time each day. If you have more time to devote, do take advantage of it.

Give your wild conure plenty of attention and you should begin to see positive results in a short time. It is very unlikely that you will purchase an untamable bird. However, if you find that you have worked for six months in the prescribed method, devoting time to the task each day without fail, and still your conure refuses to tame down, you have surely come upon an unusual, very difficult bird.

Examine your alternatives. You may opt to continue the taming lessons with more determination; this is the best choice. You may contact the pet shop from which the bird

The conure requires about two hours of lessons every day for a few weeks to really have rapid progress. When hand training your pet conure, the first drill should be in stepping onto your hand from the stand.

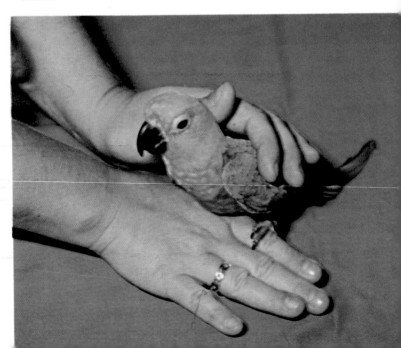

You should have the bird tame enough and trained to step onto your hand every time you offer it, otherwise you might have trouble retrieving the bird from the floor or from an unfamiliar perch.

was purchased and ask if they will consider a trade. Do not, however, *expect* the pet shop to trade your conure for a new bird; that is unrealistic.

You may even decide to build a larger cage for your conure and acquire a second bird to go with it. In this case you would not attempt to tame either bird—you can enjoy watching their interaction.

Teach your pet conure to sit on your hand and remain there before allowing it to climb onto your shoulder (see top, facing page). Conures usually like to perch on the highest perch available. Use your hand to block its climbing up your arm to your shoulder, or raise your hand higher than your shoulder (bottom, facing page). If it continues to climb, a loud "NO" might work.

One of the big tests of your bird's trust in you is how quickly it will allow you to place your hand over its back and wings.

After training your bird to go from his perch to a stick and from its perch to your hand (see photos on facing page), you can train it to go from the stick to your hand or to be petted while on your hand.

A conure that really loves you, like my model, would much rather be on my hand than on a perch, and he eagerly reaches for my finger even when on a stick which I am holding.

71

Advanced training relies heavily on your powers of observation. The model jenday conure I used stuck out one leg and would hang by this one leg from my finger (see below). I used this natural antic as a basis for many advanced trick schemes.

Advanced Training

Once the basics of tame behavior have become an established part of your conure's routine, you may consider going on to more advanced training. Conures can be taught to speak, but be prepared to spend lots of time working at it. Simple tricks can be taught also, but most people have trouble finding enough time to devote to the task.

SPEECH TRAINING

Begin speech training with simple one- or two-syllable words. "Hi" and "hello" are good words to begin with. Talk to the conure slowly and clearly. Give your lessons for five minutes throughout the day and evening. Say the word to the bird and follow it with the bird's name.

Teach only one word at a time. Do not get discouraged if

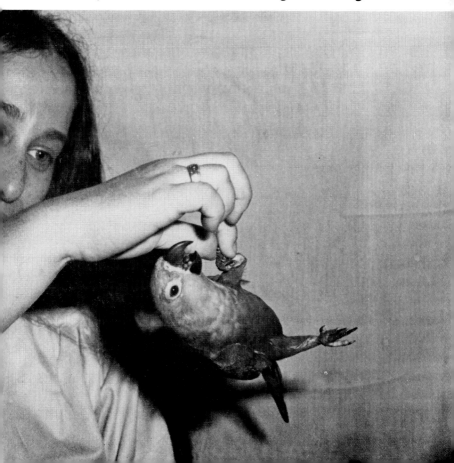

You must never try to train a conure when other birds are around. The author introduces her new conure to her macaws.

Everything seems fine and dandy. All the birds seem to ignore each other, as long as they are kept far enough apart.

But suddenly, as the conure climbs to my shoulder, the macaws, which are equally as possessive as the conure, attack the much smaller conure and, if I would not have stopped them, something serious might have happened.

75

your bird does not speak in two to three months. Some conures can be very slow learners when it comes to speech, but most do acquire a few words and sounds.

Most birds practice talking to themselves before they will try to speak to you. Listen for the first attempts when your conure is chattering as the sun sets or in the early morning. When you begin to hear formations of a word, repeat it for the bird immediately. Do not interfere with its chattering; just say the word clearly. This will help the bird practice.

Many pet shops sell recorded speech lessons for you to play on the record player. Use one of these records or use a tape of your own voice if you want, but use it only as a supplement to the live lessons.

Try to eliminate background noise during speech lessons. There is no need to darken the room or cover the bird's cage during the lesson.

Offer the bird food rewards while conducting the lessons. If your bird refuses to accept food rewards, you may try using a feeding schedule. Instead of feeding the bird in the morning, try feeding it in the afternoon, after most of your training is done for the day.

For people who work, try giving the bird one fifth of its normal ration in the morning and save the rest for training. Any food not eaten during the training session can be given to the bird when it is put back into its cage for the night.

Always give fresh water in the morning, whether or not you use a feeding schedule. *Never* skip the bird's feeding. You may feel that the bird is being stubborn, but depriving it of food will not solve the problem. You can make friends with the bird by feeding it, not by depriving it of food.

TRICK TRAINING
The sort of tricks that you may consider teaching your conure include ringing a bell on command, placing objects in a container, tightrope walking, rolling over and playing dead, among others.

Your conure must be perfectly tame if you want to take him outside. Should he fly off your hand, he must be trained to get back on your extended hand (right). If he is accustomed to taking rewards, a fresh peanut might be the way to entice him.

Playing dead is one of the favorite tricks for most parrots, but once they raise their heads (see below) it means they've had enough playing dead.

Training your pet conure to play dead is fairly easy in your hand, but trying it on your head is something else since your hair is so slippery and the conure might feel insecure. If the trick is dangerous for your conure, stop trying it or the bird will react unfavorably to all training.

To find out if a conure is really trained and tame, ask your friend or neighbor to try to "work" with your conure the same way that you do. She shouldn't have any difficulty in having the bird go from hand to perch or from stick to perch. If she does, the conure requires more training.

Observe your bird at play. What does he do naturally that you can capitalize on? Use your imagination when deciding what sort of trick to work on with the conure. Be certain to work with the bird every day. Always conduct the lessons in the same manner. Do not spend more than fifteen minutes on any one trick. Many short lessons are usually more effective than one long lesson.

Try to standardize the way in which you work with the bird; in other words use the same words and motions in each lesson. The best approach that I have found is to conduct the training sessions once an hour for five to fifteen minutes and no more. Always attempt to end the training session on a high note. For example, if you notice that your student is becoming distracted, immediately give the bird a task that you are sure it will accomplish; then end the lesson by praising the bird and offering an edible reward.

It is very important that your bird be successful in learning any task, no matter how simple. This applies to beginning taming as much as to advanced training. All creatures are motivated by success. Failure to achieve a goal is a sure way to discourage any motivation to continue.

Above all, be realistic when deciding upon a trick to teach your bird. Begin with very simple tasks and work your way up to more difficult ones. Try to limit the need for props in the first tricks.

As with beginning taming, only one person should attempt to trick-train the conure. It is hard enough to standardize your own lessons without expecting a second person to work the same way. People that do not have sufficient time to devote to trick training should not begin. Two days of training followed by two days of non-training will only confuse and discourage your conure.

Reaching your hand into a conure's cage to pull him out is a tough trick. It is better to open the cage door and offer him a peanut to come out, than to stick your hand out for him to perch on (facing page). Always allow him to walk about outside his cage (it is good exercise), but only allow him outside the cage when you are there to supervise.

If your conure sits in one place with its feathers all puffed up, you can be sure it isn't feeling well. Call your veterinarian. If he prescribes a pill, perhaps you will be lucky enough for your conure to chew it up, otherwise it will have to be dissolved in water and fed to it that way.

*First Aid
and
Illness*

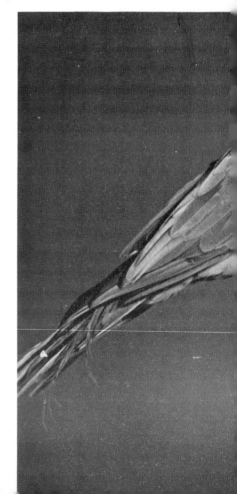

It is important for the bird owner to remember that accidents can happen, and it is often up to him or her whether the bird recovers or succumbs as a result of the accident. Accidents can be fatal, but more often than not they are treatable. They most frequently occur in beginning taming when you allow the bird freedom of the house, and from run-ins with other pets. Your conure also may fly head-first into a window or mirror, or twist a leg in a toy once thought to be safe. In an emergency, act first, and then call your vet for follow-up care. To remain calm is most important of all. The most useful first-aid preparations can be bought at your local drug store. They are hydrogen peroxide, B.F.I.

If your conure tears a claw (see facing page) and it bleeds, you must act fast.

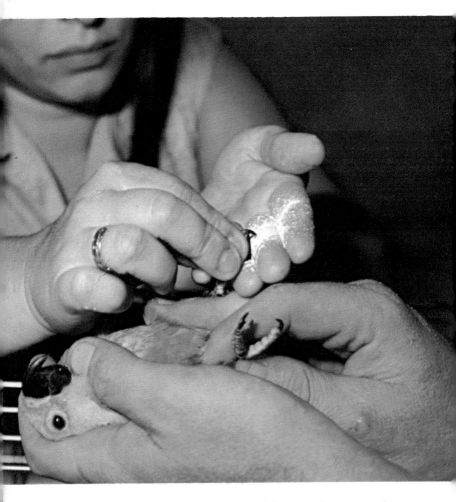

Use a styptic or antiseptic powder to stop the bleeding. Pour a generous amount onto your hand.

Then, while someone is holding the conure, apply the powder to the bleeding claw, holding it there until the bleeding stops.

antiseptic powder, Q-tips and eyewash. You may find one of the commercial bird salves useful to dress abrasions; they can be purchased at a pet shop. Use hydrogen peroxide to stop bleeding. Pour some on a dry cotton swab and squeeze out the excess. Press the swab against the bleeding spot and hold for an instant. The eyewash can be used to wash debris out of the bird's eyes, but do not spray it into the bird's nostrils.

If you suspect that your conure has broken a leg or wing, do not attempt to set the bone yourself. If the bird has a wound, carefully clean it with peroxide and keep the bird quiet. Remove any perches from the cage and keep the bird warm until you can contact a vet. Place food and water within easy reach of the bird, but do not try to force the bird to eat or drink. Place the cage in a quiet corner and let the bird rest. Partially cover the cage to keep the bird calm.

You may clip a blood feather and cause it to bleed, or you may clip a claw too short. If bleeding is light, simply place the bird back in its cage and let the blood clot. Sometimes a blood feather or a claw bleeds very heavily. If bleeding is severe, use pressure with a dry cotton swab to press against the spot. It is wise to have a styptic powder on hand for emergencies. A small amount usually will stop the flow of blood, especially if used in combination with pressure. Once bleeding abates, place the conure back in its cage and leave it in a quiet corner. Do not disturb the bird, but do watch for renewed bleeding.

The most probable cause of death in caged birds is shock, a direct result of accidental injury. The symptoms of shock are as follows: pupils that do not react to light, shallow breathing, clammy skin, soft moaning sounds and the bird's total acceptance of your touch (semiparalysis). If you suspect that the bird is suffering from shock, do not move the bird. But if there is very heavy bleeding, you must stop the flow. For birds that appear to be in shock and on which no wound is apparent, administer the following first aid.

Keep the bird warm and restrict all movement. You may find it useful to wrap the bird gently in a small cloth if it cannot keep an upright balance. Do not move the bird or take it to the vet until you have attempted first aid. Many bird owners run to the vet without any first aid to the injured pet; often this action itself causes the bird's demise. But by all means call the vet after the bird has been attended to. Learn to recognize the symptoms of shock and to respond appropriately.

Sick birds usually show symptoms of an illness long before they die. The symptoms to look out for include loss of appetite; inactivity; fluffed feathers; closed eyes or watery discharge from the eyes; sleeping all day long; standing on both feet when sleeping; clogged nasal passages or discharge; frequent sneezing; loose, watery or off-color droppings; soiling on or around the vent; and heavy, labored or irregular breathing. A bird that remains thin even though it eats a tremendous amount should also be suspected of suffering from some malady. Whenever these symptoms are seen in combination, be certain to call your vet for an appointment as soon as you can. Most illnesses can be effectively treated if you catch them in time. Do not put off visiting the vet if you expect to have your bird for many more years.

Do not attempt to administer medications that are intended for use on humans, dogs or cats unless instructed to do so by your vet. Many bird shops sell over-the-counter medications for parrot-type birds; these may help. But whenever illness is suspected, the competent, experienced vet is your best source of help.

TRAVELING WITH YOUR CONURE

You may transport a tame conure on your shoulder in the car only if the bird is a non-flyer. Be certain that your conure will not fall out the window. For untame birds the best method of transportation is a closed box with adequate ven-

Conures love to bathe. In nature they bathe in the rain, so a fine mist spray works well. Lift their wings and spray underneath them. Don't spray too closely or you might blow them off their perches.

tilation. Steady birds can be placed in a small cage on the car seat for a ride to a friend's house or a visit to the vet. When visiting your friend's home, bring along a stand for the bird to sit on when it's not on your shoulder.

It is not recommended that birds be transported in rainy weather or in winter. Trips to the park are fine for tame pets, but do not take the bird to the beach or any other place where it will be in direct sun for long periods of time.

If you are planning a vacation, you may consider taking the conure only if you plan to have adequate time to spend with it. If not, leave it with a good friend or neighbor, and be sure that the person with whom you leave the bird knows how to take care of it.

Special antibiotic ointments are available through your veterinarian to treat eye infections. The eye ring of conures is very pronounced.

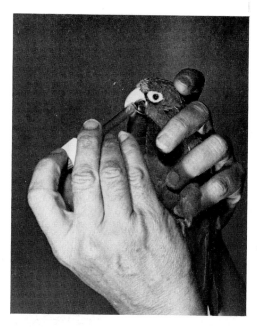

It is obvious that you should have a tame bird not only for the pleasure of its company, but so you can handle it if you have to give it medicine with an eyedropper, pull off a parasite or loose feather, or handle it just for examination.

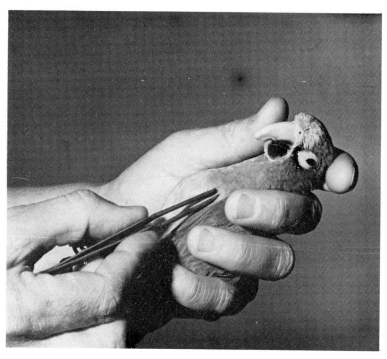